Why Revival Tarries

A Prophetic Message for Today

Matthew Robert Payne

Please visit http://personal-prophecy-today.com to sow into Matthew's writing ministry, to request a personal prophecy or life coaching, or to contact him.

Cover designed by akira007 at fiverr.com.

Edited by Lisa Thompson at www.writebylisa.com. You can email Lisa at writebylisa@gmail.com for your editing needs.

DEDICATION

To the people from my home church

Tufan:

I want to dedicate this book to Tufan, who has proven his love for me in many ways, including replacing all my furniture, buying me an expensive winter jacket, and listening to me for hours and hours. Tufan asked Jesus about me as a prophet when he first met me. Jesus said to him, "Don't treat him like a prophet and take from him, but be his friend and love him." Tufan is a valued friend of mine.

David:

I want to thank David for helping me replace my furniture. I want to thank him as an elder for asking me to teach people how to prophesy. I love you, David. I love your hunger for all that the Lord has for you.

Jinny:

I want to thank you for sharing your house and food with me. Your love is authentic, and you are a great witness to me as a pastor. You have shown me time and time again that you love me and that you value my company.

Andy:

I want to thank you for being my pastor and mentor. You have loved me as Jesus loves me, always listening to me and correcting me in love when I need correction.

Ruth:

I want to thank Ruth for her friendship and her hunger. You are a true light, and you have a lot to teach the Body of Christ in the future.

TABLE OF CONTENTS

Foreword

I contacted Matthew in July 2017 because his books changed my life. I recognized that he had insights that would be a game-changer for Christians and for the entire world if Christians put these biblically based teachings into practice. I converse with Matthew on Facebook phone calls regularly. He has proven to be a selfless and faithful friend. He clearly has the heart of the Father and has been living as Jesus taught for much of his life.

Matthew has been through the refining fire of God and has had more than his share of suffering. He truly is a beautiful person and writes solely out of his love for you. Years of experience qualify him to deliver this message, and if you are wise, you will pay attention.

After reading *Why Revival Tarries* twice, I wondered how I could write a foreword deserving of this book. Every book I have read of Matthew's— and I've read most of them—is done with excellence from start to finish. Matthew always writes his books in partnership with the Holy Spirit, and you know that you will read a high quality manuscript when you read his books.

This book is no exception. It takes a different direction and a tougher message from Matthew's other books and a hard message for people to repent if they want to be saved and if they want others to be saved.

So why hasn't this great revival, this billion-soul harvest that the prophets have predicted, come to pass yet? When will God take the world by storm and sweep across the globe with his Holy Spirit, saving millions? Matthew's answer to this might surprise you. He strongly believes that Christians need to change rather than God doing all the work for us.

This is the consuming message of this book, which shares about the importance of fulfilling the commandments of Jesus and actually practicing what the Bible says so that we are saved ourselves and are sheep, not goats. Until the church does these things and can teach new converts how to do them, revival will tarry.

As I read this book, the Holy Spirit spoke to me about ways to use my resources sacrificially to bless others and show love to people. The book is already bearing fruit.

This is the message the world has been waiting for, and you can read it. So buckle up and prepare to be challenged; it's going to be a wild ride!

Nicola Whitehall

Co-author of *Enoch Speaks from Heaven: A Divine Revelation* and of *Michael Jackson Speaks from Heaven, Book 2: A Divine Revelation*

AUTHOR'S NOTE

Before I start, I want to share that this book is my opinion and should not be taken as fact. I am a man with faults and limitations, and I have not ever attended Bible college. Some of what I say here might be error and is not infallible. I am a simple man who is largely self-taught, and this message has been burning in my heart for many years. Today the Lord, through his Holy Spirit, has directed me to release it. Throughout the text, I will include my personal beliefs and my personal findings. When I do that, I will use wording to indicate that these are my opinions, and I will put the words in italics to warn you. When you see the italics, weigh these statements carefully by the Spirt of God in you. Let God confirm them in your spirit rather than taking them as gospel fact. With this, I give you a book that was originally recorded as a video and edited and rewritten no less than three times.

This message has been on my heart for a few years. I'm quite emotional about it. I come across people all the time who talk about revival, who want revival. I don't watch the Australian news, and most of my Facebook friends live in the United States, so most of my audience is American. I write my books in American English. This book is therefore written to the American Christian, the American churchgoer. Even so, it speaks to any Christian in any nation.

I really love my pastor in Australia. God has big things planned for him. I'm with this pastor because we have similar callings on our lives. The famous preacher, Smith Wigglesworth, prophesied many years ago that the last world revival during the end times would start in Australia. It would spread through Australia, Southeast Asia, and to the rest of the world. People in Australia would be fire starters. Revivalist preachers would leave Australia and go to their birth nations and take revival there. In addition, people from around the world would fly to the Australian revival where they would be equipped, trained, and anointed. They would then return to their countries and light fires of revival. That is a promising prophecy and vision of the future.

For many years, I've known about the seven churches in the book of Revelation. Some people believe that the churches are mentioned in the order of church seasons and times and that the last church, Laodicea, describes the present time. I agree that the words about Laodicea describe the current state of the worldwide church. Our modern church is dead, and I *personally believe* that at least half of all church members are flirting with the things of the world. The world seems to be their god. They go to church each week and praise God, but I don't think that he is impressed with their so-called worship. I am reminded of this reference in the Old Testament prophetic book.

"Is not the day of the Lord darkness, and not light? Is it not very dark, with no brightness in it? 'I hate, I despise your feast days, and I do not savor your sacred assemblies. Though you offer Me burnt offerings and your grain offerings, I will not accept them, nor will I regard your fattened peace offerings. Take away from Me the noise of your songs, for I will not hear the melody of your stringed instruments. But let justice run down like water, and righteousness like a mighty stream.'" (Amos 5:20–24).

It can be really sad to be me. I have a lonely life. Although I have friends, I have only a few who actually see and understand me. I think quite deeply and am passionate about Jesus. It's hard to find people like myself. People don't understand me or see me for who I am. I've written over fifty books, and I hoped that people would learn to understand me. People who have read all my books would understand where I'm coming from, but I don't know many of those people personally and intimately.

God has blessed me with a close friend Nicola who ministers with me on my prophetic website. She knows me well and sees me. I am blessed to share my life with her. When it comes to the path of God for my life, I trust that God knows best for me.

I am different from others. I have never had a mentor to instruct or teach me. God has spoken to me and taught me all my life. I have learned everything I know about theology myself. God has led me to read books and watch videos. I have grown up to be used as a prophet and a teacher in the Body of Christ. One advantage to being self-taught is that I have learned to work things out on my own through personal revelation.

Although the leaders of many churches are blind and leading their flocks astray, they cannot lead me astray. But I could still be deceived when I teach myself, so I have friends check my books.

I *personally believe* that the church is asleep in the light. Keith Green, a popular contemporary Christian singer, wrote a song called "Asleep in the Light." If you are reading the paperback version of this book, you can search for the song on YouTube. If you are reading the Kindle version, I encourage you to stop right now and listen to the song at this link. This book expands on the message of that song.

Sadly, many churches have a reputation of being alive, but I *say personally* that in Jesus's eyes and opinion, they are actually dead. (Revelation 3:1 speaks of this.) So much of the church flirts with the things of the world and its riches, so Jesus sees them as lukewarm. (See Revelation 3:16.) It is my *personal belief* that up to 50 percent of the people who go to church each week have no idea what Jesus taught his followers to do and therefore don't even know how to be effective Christians. I *feel personally* that up to 80 percent or more of Christians cannot hear God or Jesus speak to them, and as many as 90 percent of Christians have no idea how to walk in the Spirit and be directed by God.

I *personally believe* that up to 50 percent of people who call themselves Christians will not end up in heaven when they die. Jesus says that he will vomit the lukewarm out of his mouth, and James 4:4 says that a person who is a friend of the world makes himself an enemy of God. In other words, in my *personal opinion*, if Jesus came back to take his bride in the rapture tonight, over 50 percent of the people who attend church each week would be left behind to face the tribulation. You might want to ask yourself if you are one of them.

Let's just say you had to face the tribulation. If you were left behind in the tribulation and if we looked at a scene from the future, I wonder if you would survive it. If a group of soldiers were going house to house, arresting every Christian and taking them to have their heads cut off or putting them in a FEMA camp, would you get away? If the soldiers were coming down the street and the Holy Spirit said that the only way out was to walk right through the midst of them, could you hear him say that and then obey? I *personally feel* that many church-going Christians couldn't hear the Holy Spirit give them that direction. Even those who actually heard the Holy Spirit speak might not trust that it really was the Holy Spirit and obey his direction. They might not know that angels could hide them, and they could walk right through the midst of those soldiers without being seen.

They might never have experienced that kind of supernatural life, and they would probably refuse to obey the Holy Spirit because that would mean walking straight into danger. If they didn't do what the Holy Spirit said, they'd sadly be dead if they took any other avenue. I don't know many Christians who could do it.

Could you survive if you were left behind tonight? If the Antichrist knew his time was short and he hunted down Christians, would you survive? Do you know how to survive without money? Do you know how to wait for angels or how to use your prophetic gift with other people so that they feed you? Do you have the faith for angels to turn up and feed you?

I know that you read this book to find out why revival tarries, but I first wanted to ask you to honestly look at your life and figure out if your eternal life is guaranteed. I also want you to consider if you have enough faith to endure the tribulation in case there is no rapture before the tribulation in contrast with what many teachers promise the church.

I have a *personal belief* that Jesus's return is more than twenty years away. Some people feel that they are experts and have read every book on Revelation, and they have a different opinion from mine. I know that the book of Revelation is one of the most misunderstood books in the world, and everyone seems to have their own opinion about it. I know that people like to argue, and you are free to comment on this book and say that this is not true.

Many prophecies have been spoken over my life. If I started today, it would take up to twenty years to fulfill them all. I have been pushed to a point four times when I considered taking my own life, and I don't feel that Jesus kept me alive all those times not to fulfill the promises he has made over my life.

I know an apostle in India who is met on his birthday every year by Jesus in the flesh. This has happened for the last twenty years on his birthday. I don't know many people who have met Jesus in the flesh. This man was also saved by Jesus in the flesh. Jesus come to him as a man, led him to himself, and said, "I'm the Messiah. I'm the Jesus you're looking for." Jesus led him to himself, baptized him in a pool of water, and then baptized him in the Holy Spirit and fire. The man had to go and sleep in a cool well for forty days because his skin was burning so much after he was baptized in fire.

This man promised Jesus that he'd plant fifteen hundred churches. Well, he's only planted six hundred churches so far in twenty years. He probably would have more churches by now, but he relies on the West to give him the finances to build churches. He has many churches with congregations that simply have no church buildings. They meet in homes and out in the open. When it's raining on Sunday, they don't have church. He's been in ministry for twenty years, and he has nine hundred churches left to build before his promise to Jesus can be fulfilled. I think I would trust that his promise will be fulfilled as he has been meeting

Jesus in the flesh every year for the last two decades. I would trust him over any pastor or preacher who thinks he has fresh insight on the book of Revelation.

I see a lot of people talking about revival in the end times and the rapture and the like, and they have no idea of God's times and seasons. I hear people talk about revival, and they believe that is the answer for the world. I *personally believe* that they are wrong.

The answer is you.

You are supposed to feed the hungry, bless the poor, and encourage the broken-hearted. I *personally believe* that the Body of Christ should be meeting the needs of everyone now, not at some magical time in the future. The Bible already tells people how to do it.

Sadly, I see many Christians talking the talk, but I don't see Christians walking the walk. I've lived for years and years and associated with many Christians. Maybe I've been associating with the wrong kind of Christians. But almost every Christian I know has walked past homeless people. When I've been with Christians and a homeless person is desperate enough to come into McDonald's and ask every single person there for spare change, everyone, including the Christians, turned him away without giving him change. Oh, they had money. In fact, later that night, they bought more food or coffee. But they refuse to give to the poor.

The homeless person only begs like that when they're really desperate. They really need a hit, or they really need some alcohol to make it through the winter's night. They have very painful withdrawals coming on, so they're desperate and begging for money. It takes humility to beg.

Christians give excuses and tell themselves, "He's a heroin addict. I don't want to give him money. He'll spend it on drugs." The fact is that a heroin addict could break into your house, steal your TV, take it to a pawn shop, and sell it. He could plan his actions, case your house, check out your schedule, wipe out your house, and sell everything at a second-hand dealer.

He'd give his ID to the second-hand dealer as required by law, and he'd get his money. Then he'd buy heroin and shoot it up his arm for three days. That's what a sophisticated heroin addict does. Other heroin addicts mug or rob people. Others sell their girlfriends as prostitutes. The really honest ones, the ones with a good heart who have so much personal pain that they're addicted to drugs, the really honest ones, beg. They go to every single person and cry and beg for help.

Most Christians who I have associated with in the past simply refuse to give to these poor souls. I *personally believe* that even the homeless who are not heroin addicts or alcoholics don't receive a second glance from the majority of people in the church.

Jesus said this in Luke 6:30. "Give to everyone who asks of you. And from him who takes away your goods do not ask them back."

You can see that Jesus tells his followers, us believers, to give to *everyone* who asks for money. He goes on to say that even if the sophisticated heroin addict steals from you, do not do anything about it.

So if the sophisticated drug addict steals your TV, Jesus says even if you know about it, don't press charges. Don't ask for it back. He really needs the money, so let him steal from you.

And regarding the honest drug addict who comes and begs, Jesus says, "Give to everybody who asks of you." The homeless beg, and I *personally believe* that most Christians refuse to give. Besides the heroin addict who begs, others need money too: the poor, the homeless, the broken, and people overseas who are starving. They're dying because the Christian church will not give. The Christian church is spending it on their brand-new cars and their brand-new fashions and their two hundred and fifty dollar dresses and their eighty dollar jeans. They won't give. The church at large, I *personally believe,* is dead.

In Revelation, the message to the church of Laodicea addresses the lukewarm church (Revelation 3:14–21). The passage very candidly speaks of people who are rich but who have need of nothing. They might sing to Jesus, but they certainly don't show him their love by obeying him. So many Christians don't know that Jesus commanded you to give to everybody who asks of you. That means that every time you refuse that beggar on the street, you are saying no to Jesus's command, and you are disobeying Jesus. People have their excuses and reasons for not giving to the poor. "He is a drug addict; he's a drunk, and I'm not going to enable him." On one hand, you say you love Jesus, yet on the other hand, you blatantly disobey him through your manmade traditions and excuses.

I can hear Jesus saying this in Matthew 15:8–9. "'These people draw near to Me with their mouth, and honor Me with their lips, but their heart is far from Me. And in vain they worship Me, teaching as doctrines the commandments of men.'"

When people refuse the person who begs with supposed justifications of their actions, they are listening to the doctrines of men that Jesus referred to here.

In Matthew 5:44, Jesus commanded, "Bless your enemies." I see people get into a Facebook fight with fifty or a hundred posts. People are swearing at each other, calling each other names, and behaving badly. Christians act like this and then say "Bless you" to each other at the end of the argument. They think that's what Jesus meant by blessing your enemies. So many people have called me names and all sorts of things because I've actually bothered to try and correct someone. I spend some time trying to talk some reason into a person, and I just can't be talked around. At the end of the argument, after they've called me all sorts of names and said their piece, they say, "Bless you" and think they're obeying Jesus's command. I *personally believe* that is not blessing your enemy. Colossians 3:12 says, "Therefore, as the elect of God, holy and beloved, put on tender mercies, kindness, humility, meekness, longsuffering."

The person has just proven, with their insults and all their arguments, that they disobey this standard in Scripture. At the end, they say "bless you," thinking they're blessing their enemy. But when they do that, they're saying that I have become their enemy, because I'm actually trying to point something out to them.

Do you know how I *personally believe* you bless your enemy? If you're having a problem with someone at work and they're really making it hard for you, go and buy a movie voucher for ten visits. Get a hundred dollar movie voucher and give it to them. Tell them, "I know we're not seeing eye to eye, but everyone loves the movies. I've bought you this. I hope you enjoy it. Think of me when you're watching your movies. We really got into it yesterday, but no harm done. Enjoy the movies." I *personally believe* that's how to bless your enemies. That's how to bless your enemies. That's what Jesus is talking about.

Your former enemies will find it really hard to be against you after you do that, but it'll cost you to do it. I *personally believe* that blessing your enemies should always cost you. When a pastor preaches at a church and you give him a blessing, it costs; it costs money. Don't have an argument with someone and say "God bless you" afterwards because you think you are obeying Jesus by saying it.

Many people think of this passage in Romans 12:18–21 when they encounter enemies. "If it is possible, as much as depends on you, live peaceably with all men. Beloved, do not avenge yourselves, but rather give place to wrath; for it is written, 'Vengeance is Mine, I will repay,' says the Lord. Therefore 'if your enemy is hungry, feed him; if he is thirsty, give him a drink; for in so doing you will heap coals of fire on his head.' Do not be overcome by evil, but overcome evil with good."

People think by feeding their enemy, giving them food, and then blessing them, they're actually going to torture their enemy. Many Christians go out of their way to be nice to an enemy, hoping that their kindness will torture them. But people don't understand what this verse means in its cultural context.

This verse relates to this story. In a Jewish village, a man used to stay up all night and tend a fire. In the morning, he'd put all the hot coals into an urn on his head. Then he'd take that urn around the village to every woman and give them some coals to start their fire in the morning.[1]

Paul was using a relevant cultural example that the people of his day understood. Paul was saying, "If you have an enemy, bless him so much that he'll become the person who stays up all night and blesses your whole village."

---

[1] Clyde L. Pilkington Jr, "Heaping Coals of Fire: A Figure of Speech," *Daily Goodies* (blog), January 4, 2010, https://dailygoodies.wordpress.com/2010/01/04/heaping-coals-of-fire-a-figure-of-speech/.

Many times, you will start off with someone in your life as an enemy. But this person will later bring real breakthrough and be a real covenant partner with you and really work well with you in ministry. Satan knows in advance who is significant and who will make a major impact in your life. Often the enemy starts one of your relationships with difficulty. Paul says to persist through that and be nice to your enemy. You'll turn him around, and he'll be the biggest blessing in your life.

I *personally believe* that the people of God ignore the poor and the homeless. They make enemies and keep them through wrong beliefs and wrong teachings. The modern Christian is lukewarm and is in love with the world and its lusts. The blind lead the blind in the modern church, and somehow they want a revival of God to come and fix everything. I don't *think personally* that revival will change the systemic problems.

I hear many people speak about revival, but I *personally believe* that it's selfishness. The church is selfish. They just want God to save everyone. They just want expansion in the church; they just want everyone saved, and they want the Holy Spirit to come down in such a visitation that all the work is done. I *personally believe* that if they really cared for the non-Christians, they'd learn how to heal and prophesy and bless non-Christians financially. They would help everyone. If they truly knew Jesus, they would be doing the works of the kingdom. Everyone would be!

I *personally believe* if the churches knew how to train and equip people, everyone would be equipped to heal, to prophesy, and to make a real difference. If Christians knew that they were making themselves an enemy of God by loving the world and buying all the world's goods and services for themselves as James 4:4 says, Christians would be a lot freer in their giving.

I saw this in an article on the internet from "Relevant Magazine."

"The truth is: Giving is a heart issue, not a money issue.

When Paul spoke about the legendary giving of the Macedonian church he urged the Corinthian church to prove their love like the Macedonians proved theirs: 'But as you abound in everything—in faith, in speech, in knowledge, in all diligence, and in your love for us—see that you abound in this grace also. I speak not by commandment, but I am testing the sincerity of your love by the diligence of others' (2 Corinthians 8:7–8)."[2]

The same article had this to say about tithing.

"Tithers make up only 10–25 percent of a normal congregation. Only 5 percent of the United States tithes with 80 percent of Americans only giving 2 percent of their income."[3]

I *personally believe* that the Holy Spirit told me years ago that most of the problems in the world could be solved if people weren't selfish. If the selfishness were taken out of the Christian church, if the people in the Christian church weren't selfish anymore and didn't live for themselves first, but were willing to share as Paul encourages us to, I *personally believe* that we would have a much greater effect in evangelizing the world.

"Command those who are rich in this present age not to be haughty, nor to trust in uncertain riches but in the living God, who gives us richly all

Mike Holmes, "What Would Happen if the Church Tithed?" Relevant Magazine, March 8, 2016, https://relevantmagazine.com/love-and-money/what-would-happen-if-church-tithed.
Ibid.

things to enjoy. Let them do good, that they be rich in good works, ready to give, willing to share, storing up for themselves a good foundation for the time to come, that they may lay hold on eternal life" (1 Timothy 6:17–19).

You might read the above passage and say to yourself that you are not rich. But compared to living on two dollars a day that many in the world are living on, you are indeed rich. Even if you are on government benefits, you are considered rich by the world's standards.

I have lived with few friends and with no mentors. That has led me to search out answers for myself, and I often just work things out by using common sense. How can a selfish church that won't give make any lasting change in the world that they claim to want to save? And when the people do come to church through revival, what lessons will we teach them if we don't live as Jesus taught us?

It is so sad. People talk about revival as though it's the answer to the problems of the world. I *personally feel* that this way of thinking is strange. Do you know when you say "We want a revival," you mean that we're dead and we need to be revived? The meaning of revived is coming back from the dead. It means you've passed out, and you're dead, and you've been resuscitated and revived. I *personally feel* that when the church cries out for revival, they're actually saying, "God we're dead; we need your touch." It's a very bad confession when you think of it in those terms.

Maybe you are not as deep of a thinker as I am about these subjects. The church of Philadelphia is mentioned just before the church of Laodicea. Let's focus our attention on what the Bible says about that church now in Revelation 3:7–13.

> *"And to the angel of the church in Philadelphia write, 'These things says He who is holy, He who is true, "He who has the key of David, He who opens and no one shuts, and shuts and no one opens": "I know your works. See, I have set before you an open door, and no one can shut it; for you have a little strength, have kept My word, and have not denied My name. Indeed I will make those of the synagogue of Satan, who say they are Jews and are not, but lie—indeed I will make them come and worship before your feet, and to know that I have loved you. Because you have kept My command to persevere, I also will keep you from the hour of trial which shall come upon the whole world, to test those who dwell on the earth.*

Behold, I am coming quickly! Hold fast what you have, that no one may take your crown. He who overcomes, I will make him a pillar in the temple of My God, and he shall go out no more. I will write on him the name of My God and the name of the city of My God, the New Jerusalem, which comes down out of heaven from My God. And I will write on him My new name. "He who has an ear, let him hear what the Spirit says to the churches."

This following is what I *personally believe*. You can read more about this subject in my book, *Optimistic Visions of Revelation*. When God wants to move one last time, he will use people who qualify as Philadelphians. He will use Philadelphian pastors, people who have a heart like this passage. He will find people like this church that was prophesied over by John. They will be people who he can find no fault in, people with little strength running churches, and those who are shepherds all over the world. They will teach and equip their people how to love. Their congregation will be out in the streets, saving the lost. The churches will have an outward focus and a mission to bless others who don't attend their church. They will be beautiful people, and he will teach all those who go to these churches how to do all the following:

- love others

- endure with people

- be patient

- sow

- give and

- be a real Christian.

Jesus will raise up these churches. He will slowly bring all these Philadelphian pastors to the forefront. Every city, every town, will have a Philadelphian pastor. The Holy Spirit will raise up all these leaders and church bodies who know how to love. He will then pour out this revival and bring in all the harvest. The people will only come to these special churches.

In my *personal opinion*, most of the church—all the religious church, those who aren't obeying, those with pastors who aren't Philadelphian pastors—will not see the effect of the revival. Only the Philadelphian churches will grow.

I *personally believe* that the anointing and the presence of God will leave these big churches, and they'll be ghost towns. Multimillion dollar buildings just won't have people coming to them anymore.

All the Philadelphian pastors will talk and network together. They'll become a church that the religious establishment will call a cult. Jesus spoke about this when he said:

"'Blessed are those who are persecuted for righteousness' sake, For theirs is the kingdom of heaven. Blessed are you when they revile and persecute you, and say all kinds of evil against you falsely for My sake'" (Matthew 5:10–11).

The religious church will call this church a cult. Jesus speaks about these religious churches and their leaders in our key passage in Revelation 3:9. "Indeed I will make those of the synagogue of Satan, who say they are Jews and are not, but lie—indeed I will make them come and worship before your feet, and to know that I have loved you."

The new churches will be rejected by the mainstream churches, but they'll be on fire. They'll build, equip, and train people to be fire starters and to preach a message of holiness and repentance. Their preachers will preach a message that brings conviction and repentance.

As the Spirit of the Lord takes hold in the revival, those people will come out of those churches and go all around the world and preach repentance and revival. The whole world will light up, and all the people will flood into those churches, and then the end will come.

I currently attend a church that knows how to love. People in the church love me, embrace my gifts, acknowledge me as a prophet, and put me to work teaching their people how to prophesy and witness on the streets. People in that church came to my house and totally replaced all my furniture at no cost. People in the church saw that I had not spent much money on my own personal clothing, so they bought me expensive clothes. My pastor has recognized my teaching gift and has released me to preach in his pulpit. In the past few weeks, we have had some seriously afflicted people coming to our church who are quite raw and hard for people to accept. They have been warmly loved and embraced. God is looking for churches where anyone fits in and is loved and encouraged.

It is my *personal belief* that at the moment, most churches don't know how to love people who are not nice and respectable. Most churches today don't have people who operate in their gifts apart from those on the stage each week. Most Christians don't know the fifty commands of Jesus and that Jesus actually had fifty commands that he wanted his followers to obey as they follow him.[4] Most Christians today don't know how to walk in the Spirit, how to hear from Jesus, how to be directed by Jesus or the Holy Spirit, or how to obey Jesus. What I have mentioned is not high and mighty or just for special Christians. These matters are fundamental to the Christian life, and if people are not walking in them, how can they possibly have a revival and then correctly disciple others in the faith?

I *personally feel* that many people want the rapture to come. People want revival to break out; they want the last days to happen. People want to go home in the rapture because living on earth these days is becoming too hard for them. They feel that it's getting too dark. Everyone wants to leave earth. They want the revival and the outpouring to be over so that everyone can be saved, and they can go home to heaven.

---

[4] Matthew Robert Payne, "The Fifty Commands of Jesus," *Ezine Articles*, February 26, 2007, http://ezinearticles.com/?The-Fifty-Commands-of-Jesus&id=468177.

I'm amazed that so many people don't know that there will be an outpouring, a major harvest, before the rapture. Many people think that the rapture will be tomorrow, and they follow the blood moons and think that the rapture will happen soon.

Every year, someone seems to say "This is the end." Many people are convinced that we're in the last two or five or ten years. They have no idea that God might want to save a billion souls before Jesus comes back. At the rate we are going, it looks like he won't come back at all!

Now let me share something that I feel is significant to this teaching. When it hasn't rained for years, the land becomes dead and dry with cracks in the soil. You have seen the ground like that before. So when it rains and pours and the rain comes down in torrents, all the water runs off and doesn't soak in.

personally feel that the modern church is dead. The people aren't equipped and aren't working in their gifts. If you disagree with my statement that the church is dead, compare the modern church with the church in the book of Acts. When you contemplate the church in Acts, check to see if your current church is anything like that. I *personally believe* that 80 percent of those in church can't hear from God. The church doesn't know how to love people, and they have proven it to me.

If it rained in revival right now, all the water would run off. What would happen if stadium revivals started now and stadiums in each city in the United States lit up with many people saved? New converts would spend one or two weeks in church and realize that Christians are hypocrites and that Christians don't love them.

The new converts would find that the church can't handle Stephen holding hands with his gay lover in church. They don't realize that it will take him a few years to come out of homosexuality. The modern church does not have the patience for a heroin addict who will take more than one revival meeting to recover from his addiction. If he is miraculously set free from his physical addiction, does the church have the love and patience that it will take for him to be healed of his past emotional and spiritual wounds, past sexual abuse, and all the trauma he has suffered in life?

The pain just won't go away. The new converts have to address the emotional roots of that pain. I have *found personally* that the modern church doesn't seem to care. In the modern church, you have to pay to see a counselor; it's not free anymore. I know all this because I have been sexually abused, had sex addictions, have had alter personalities, have had demonic issues, and have had to pay counselors to receive my freedom.

How will all these messed up people stay in church? Even to navigate a church today, you have to speak Christianese. We throw around the word anointing so easily, but someone who's not a Christian and even a Christian who is not a Pentecostal doesn't know what the anointing is. Most Christians don't really know what the anointing is or understand how it works.

I bought a whole book by a very well-known Christian minister on the anointing to learn what the anointing was, but it didn't teach me anything. I wanted to know what the anointing was and how to move in it. This leader obviously moves in the anointing and sees many salvations and miracles at his meetings, so I thought he'd know about it. He wrote a book about it, but I didn't learn anything. I knew most of it.

Christians toss around so many words: deliverance, grace, favor, anointing, and similar words. How will a new convert understand what we are saying even if they want to know?

Another factor is often overlooked when people speak of revival. The average person, it is said, needs many encounters with the gospel before they will make a decision for Christ. How will we have a harvest when not many people in the church share the gospel with their friends even once? To have a harvest, you need to plant a seed first.

How can you bring in a harvest if a seed wasn't planted? Everyone in the world needs seed given to them before it's harvested. People, we need to change. We need to learn how to be a living witness for Jesus everywhere we are. If you are a great witness for Christ, this scenario might not apply to you, but only people who are a strong witness can relate to this.

The seed can be harvested at a revival meeting, but your work friends will only ever come to a revival meeting because you've been such a beautiful friend to them. If they trust you, you can invite them to a meeting. You can tell them that someone important is coming to town and they need to be there. They will take your word for it because you're such a beautiful Christian and different from others they've known. You might be the first Christian who actually listened to them and was with them when their husband left them while they cried. You shared what you do at church and about the exciting life you have as a Christian. You are the first person that ever listened to them and loved them, and you don't seem religious like all the other Christians. You don't seem like a hypocrite because they've tested you, swore at you, poked you, and annoyed you, yet you kept on coming back and loving and forgiving them.

They might not have ever met anyone like you, and they want what you have. That means you've planted a seed. So when I come to town and I'm a big shot in fifteen years' time, you can tell them, "Come and meet my friend, Matthew. I've been reading his books for years, and he's coming to town to preach at this conference. Please come with me. Remember,

I always talk about him. He's coming to town; you have to come and meet him because I'm going to hear him."

And they think, "Well, I'll come for them. It's really important to them, so I'll come because I love this person. They've been really good to me. Sure, I'll come and listen to their hero."

Seeds have to be planted, and the seed for a massive worldwide revival simply hasn't been planted yet. Christian TV isn't converting nearly the numbers of people who need to be saved. Only Christians listen to it. Christians are just preaching to each other.

I recently heard that a country in South America had a crusade for five days. It was huge, and all the churches came together to put the crusade on. They filled this stadium, and Christians met, praised God, and had revival meetings. People were touched and blessed by God and enjoyed themselves.

The evangelistic team did a follow up a month later, and not one person had become a Christian. Not one of the churches had grown even by one member as a result of the crusade! The massive meeting and expense by the churches bore no fruit with no new people coming to the churches. This preacher questioned, "Why are we even doing this? It's bearing no fruit." Many times, only Christians attend these outpourings. Christians are preaching to other Christians.

I *personally believe* that the world needs you. The world needs you to obey Jesus, plant all the seeds, and learn to be equipped now. You need to find a church that's using everyone in their gifts and become part of it. Learn some things and witness to every single person you meet. You have to learn how to do it. I have written three books that can help steer you in the right direction.

- *Prophetic Evangelism Made Simple*
- *Influencing Your World for Christ* and
- *13 Tips to Becoming the Light of Christ.*

You will not save the world by following popular YouTube preachers, studying theology, and going to church. If the church, as big as it is worldwide, is not teaching people how to love, how to minister in their gifts, how to win people to Christ, or how to be an effective witness to others, what use would it be if we had a revival? Sure, the church, full of Christians, would flock to it for a fresh touch from the Lord, but where would the dying and suffering people of the world be? The homeless man would still be begging in your street, and the heroin addict would still be shooting up!

That is why revival tarries. That's why it hasn't hit, because we don't have churches that can disciple and love people into wholeness. If it rains right now, the water would all run off. I *personally believe* the church might grow 10 to 20 percent, but the majority of people saved would leave the church because they wouldn't find love there.

If you read the parable of the sower, you will find that the cares of the world and the deceitfulness of riches choked out the seed, and it was unfruitful in their lives. This applies to most Christians I have known. "Now he who received seed among the thorns is he who hears the word, and the cares of this world and the deceitfulness of riches choke the word, and he becomes unfruitful" (Matthew 13:22).

The first two seeds, the one that fell on the wayside and the one that was sown among stony ground, represent most of the people who would be saved in a revival today. If they are like the average Christian, they would become unfruitful because money and the cares of the world would become an idol. I *personally believe* that very few new converts would grow so that they experience thirty, sixty, and a hundredfold increase.

I have to ask you how many people are Christians this year because of you? How many people did you lead to the Lord this year? I led two people to the Lord two weeks ago, and six months before that, we led another two people to the Lord. I'm working with a pastor who's more of an evangelist, and I'm more of a prophet. For years and years, I've prophetically evangelized and planted seeds in people. Now I plant the seed through prophecy, and my pastor and I harvest some of the seed. Sometimes the Holy Spirit says, "These people are ready to come to the Lord."

Most people aren't ready. According to studies, most people need six presentations of the gospel before they come to the Lord.

An internet article by Tim Brister says:

"It has been discovered by researchers that the *average* number of times a person will hear the gospel before they come to faith in Christ is 5-6 times. If that is the case, then it makes sense why churches are not growing by conversion growth. We aren't sowing the seed!"[5]

Did you know that? Did you know that before someone can come to the Lord, they have to hear the gospel an average of six times? Do you share the gospel with people you know?

The youth in America at university are in training to become socialists and Democrats. We need change in the leadership at universities. The false prophets, the professors at universities, are teaching people how to be socialist Democrats. What will you do? You can have your revival, but all your youth will still be indoctrinated with that garbage.

And what about your government? Donald was elected by God with a miracle, and half the Christian church doesn't even think he is of God.

---

[5] Tim Brister, "Sow the Seed!" *Tim Brister* (blog), August 22, 2011, http://timmybrister.com/2011/08/sow-the-seed/.

These people that reject your president couldn't hear from God if God hit them on the head. Many in the church, so many Christians, can't see that President Trump was selected and appointed by God. But they think their government can save them. The Christians have to influence every sphere of society; it can't be just done in the mountain of the church.

Do you know how to disciple a person? If someone became a Christian, do you know how to teach him how to be an effective Christian? Do you actually know how to be an effective Christian yourself? I *feel personally* that 90 percent of you have never heard of the fifty commandments of Jesus.

If you go to a foreign country or a new suburb, if you're driving down unfamiliar roads, you might feel anxious until you find out the speed limit. When you know the speed limit, you relax because you know that you're not breaking the law if you stay under the speed limit. But when you go somewhere unfamiliar, you need to find the speed limit sign so that you can obey it. The sign tells you how to obey the law.

How do you think you can obey Jesus's commands when you don't even know them? Jesus said this in John 14:21: "He who has My commandments and keeps them, it is he who loves Me. And he who loves Me will be loved by My Father, and I will love him and manifest Myself to him."

Jesus said in this passage that if you say you love him, then you should obey his commandments. You don't know how to obey them if you don't know them. Four times in the Gospel of John, Jesus said if you love me, obey my commandments. (See John 14:15, 21, 23, and John 15:10.) These were the words of Jesus between the Last Supper and the crucifixion just before he died. Why don't pastors teach on these commands? You can find a list of them here. The apostle John thought the commandments of Jesus were important and needed to be obeyed, so he instructed his followers to obey them three extra times in his letters to the church.

Consider that these fifty commands that I have spoken about form the meat in the sandwich that Jesus was teaching.[6] You might find that you

---

[6] Payne, "The Fifty Commands of Jesus," http://ezinearticles.com/?The-Fifty-Commands-of-Jesus&id=468177.

have been living your life as a foolish man who built his house on the sand. Jesus explains clearly that if you hear what he taught and you don't do it, you are foolish.

> "Therefore whoever hears these sayings of Mine, and does them, I will liken him to a wise man who built his house on the rock: and the rain descended, the floods came, and the winds blew and beat on that house; and it did not fall, for it was founded on the rock.

> "But everyone who hears these sayings of Mine, and does not do them, will be like a foolish man who built his house on the sand: and the rain descended, the floods came, and the winds blew and beat on that house; and it fell. And great was its fall" (Matthew 7:24–27).

Do you honestly think you've built your life on the rock? I know some people who really follow me and who read my books and are intentional in how they live. They have built their lives on the rock, but how can you say you've built your life on the rock when you don't even know what Jesus taught you? How can you obey it? I used one illustration about giving money to the homeless, and most of you don't know that was a commandment. So how were you obeying it? Most of you are disobeying it and using commandments and ideas of men to say no to these people. Giving to all who ask of you is simply one out of fifty commandments that you don't observe.

You probably didn't know how to bless your enemies because you think blessing your enemies means that you say "bless you" after you have a Facebook fight. But blessing your enemy means buying him or her a one hundred dollar movie voucher or something similar. That's how you bless them; that's how you change the situation.

Giving to the homeless who ask you for money and blessing your enemies are just two commands. Jesus had fifty! Do I need to go through all of them to convince you? I *believe personally* that the church isn't ready for a bigger church now because the established church isn't even obeying what Jesus taught his followers to do.

Why does the Holy Spirit need to visit us in power in a revival anyway? You have the Holy Spirit in you; why don't you shine like a light? Jesus said:

"You are the light of the world. A city that is set on a hill cannot be hidden. Nor do they light a lamp and put it under a basket, but on a lampstand, and it gives light to all who are in the house. Let your light so shine before men, that they may see your good works and glorify your Father in heaven" (Matthew 5:14–16).

Sadly, most of you are hiding your light under a basket, too afraid of what your co-workers will say if you bring up Jesus and share the gospel. You're afraid that you'll get in trouble and lose your job for talking to people about salvation. You are more afraid of losing your job or of being rejected than of that person going to hell.

You pray that someone can save your family because you've bashed them so much with your religion, your opinions, and your lack of love. They won't listen to you anymore, and you want someone like me to come along and give your family a prophetic word and totally rock their world and bring them to Christ. You need someone else to come and save your family, and you're praying for them. You're really sad for those in your family who aren't saved, and you know someone has to save them. But who do you think will save your family when no one seems to be sharing the gospel these days? You won't go out of your comfort zone to save someone else's family. You don't care about someone else's family. You think you will lose your job if you witness to that person at work.

Someone is praying for that work colleague of yours and hoping that someone will witness to them, and you don't know it, but you are supposed to be the answer to that prayer. You are in his or her life every day, but you won't open your mouth or shine your light. You've hidden your light under a basket.

Jesus told the parable of the talents in Matthew 25:14–30:

"For the kingdom of heaven is like a man traveling to a far country, who called his own servants and delivered his goods to them. And to one he gave five talents, to another two, and to another one, to each according to his own ability; and immediately he went on a journey. Then he who had received the five talents went and traded with them, and made another five talents. And likewise he who had received two gained two more also. But he who had received one went and dug in the

ground, and hid his lord's money. After a long time the lord of those servants came and settled accounts with them.

"So he who had received five talents came and brought five other talents, saying, 'Lord, you delivered to me five talents; look, I have gained five more talents besides them.' His lord said to him, 'Well done, good and faithful servant; you were faithful over a few things, I will make you ruler over many things. Enter into the joy of your lord.' He also who had received two talents came and said, 'Lord, you delivered to me two talents; look, I have gained two more talents besides them.' His lord said to him, 'Well done, good and faithful servant; you have been faithful over a few things, I will make you ruler over many things. Enter into the joy of your lord.'

"Then he who had received the one talent came and said, 'Lord, I knew you to be a hard man, reaping where you have not sown, and gathering where you have not scattered seed. And I was afraid, and went and hid your talent in the ground. Look, there you have what is yours.'

47

"But his lord answered and said to him, 'You wicked and lazy servant, you knew that I reap where I have not sown, and gather where I have not scattered seed. So you ought to have deposited my money with the bankers, and at my coming I would have received back my own with interest. So take the talent from him, and give it to him who has ten talents.

'For to everyone who has, more will be given, and he will have abundance; but from him who does not have, even what he has will be taken away. And cast the unprofitable servant into the outer darkness. There will be weeping and gnashing of teeth.'

I am not sure if you have ever noticed this, but the person who was given one talent and did not invest it and bring a return to the Master was thrown into the outer darkness where there will be weeping and gnashing of teeth. Many people believe in the popular hyper-grace message that says once you are saved, you are always saved. In effect, this is saying that a Christian cannot go to hell.

People who have been taught this error don't believe that they could ever go to a place where there will be weeping and gnashing of teeth. They do not think that they could ever find themselves in this position personally as this last servant, who did not do anything with his talent. We have discussed that few people know what Jesus taught. We have shared that few people can hear the voice of Jesus, even though Jesus says quite clearly that his sheep hear his voice and follow him. We have shared that many Christians allow the cares of this world to choke out the Word, and they are unfruitful. Are you fruitful or not?

A popular teacher that I follow says that a large percentage of listeners go forward when he gives an altar call for those who don't know their life purpose and who want God to show them. Therefore, I know that a majority of you who are reading this book—Christians—do not know your life purpose. If you have been given a talent to serve God with your life and you don't know what that talent is, how can you expect to ever invest it, like the man who had five talents or even two talents? Will you face the Master one day with no idea of if your life was ever fruitful?

I *personally believe* that many of you readers do know what you should be doing with your life, but life has gotten in the way, and you have refused to obey the call on your life.

Three books that can help you with this subject are:

- *Driven by Eternity* by John Bevere
- *Living for Eternity* by Matthew Robert Payne and
- *Finding your Purpose in Christ* by Matthew Robert Payne.

When a restaurant becomes very successful, the owners sometimes wish to expand. Each restaurant can only be open at certain times and can only seat a maximum number of people during the dinner rush hour. The owner might find another location and open another restaurant under the same name to increase his profits. Now he can serve twice as many customers during peak times.

The restaurant owner or an entrepreneur who values the restaurant might decide to franchise his restaurant and sell the rights to opening one of his restaurants in other cities in the nation or world. Before a restaurant can become a franchise, however, it must have effective methods, food preparation, and policies to ensure success in any environment. These systems, along with the correct procedures, training, and the reputation of the restaurant franchise, assure future owners success in their endeavour. Fast food restaurants, including McDonalds, Wendy's, and KFC, have used this model, as well as family establishments, such as Chili's, Applebee's, and Red Robin. Even some expensive restaurants have built chains through these methods.

Before Jesus can franchise his church, before he can save the world in a last days outpouring and revival, he has to get the model right. He has to have churches known for their faith and their love. He needs churches filled with Christians who know how to obey him and that are teaching what he taught. He needs his people to know him intimately and know how to be led by his Holy Spirit. He needs his people equipped to work within their gifting and operating as led by the Holy Spirit each day and not churches only run by the people on the platforms. He needs a church that will accept people from the highways and byways.

The church needs to learn how to love correctly. Heidi Baker, the famous preacher and missionary, has a message where she says, "Stop for the one." I've only heard her preach twice in person, and both times, she powerfully impacted my life. I *personally think* that 95 percent of the people who hear Heidi love what she's doing and wish they could be like her. But they don't pay close attention to what she says or do it. They hear her and want to be like her. They think that she's a wonderful person to book for conferences, but they don't stop for the one. She says to stop for the one in front of you. She says, "Do you want to know how to minister to people? Minister to the person God puts in front of you."

This is what she does in her personal ministry; she stops for the one in front of her. If she's walking out of an airport and a homeless person, a beggar, comes up to her, she stops and ministers to that person's need. I've personally seen her do this on a YouTube video. Wherever she goes, she stops. Her message is to stop for the one. But I *personally believe* that most Christians have heard of her and they might have heard her preach that message, but they simply don't do what she says.

I estimate that maybe a hundred people will watch this video or up to a thousand people will read this book over the next few years. But I could ask every one of you hundred people who watch this to share this video with all your friends. I know that not more than two or three of you will do it. Is it because I'm not convincing you? Or is it because you're afraid of what your friends will think if you share it?

So many people write to me and send me messages. They want me to listen to a video and pass it along to my friends. I don't send any videos to my friends, not because I don't care, but I just don't have the time to watch them all and do it.

If a close friend sends me something, I look at the video because they know that I don't like to be interrupted. If they send me something, it must be important. I look at it and often share it.

But honestly when people send videos and say, "Send this to all your friends and send one back to me," I don't do that. I am personally taught by the Holy Spirit.

I suppose I bring a different message than most messages you hear. Leaders have tried to bring revival through prayer movements, calls to prayer, and movements to bring together many people in the United States. But I *personally believe*, it's enough. They've tried enough to bring revival.

God said this once in Amos 5:20–24. I have quoted it already in this book, but I will share it again for you to read.

"Is not the day of the Lord darkness, and not light? Is it not very dark, with no brightness in it? 'I hate, I despise your feast days, and I do not savor your sacred assemblies. Though you offer Me burnt offerings and your grain offerings, I will not accept them, nor will I regard your fattened peace offerings. Take away from Me the noise of your songs, for I will not hear the melody of your stringed instruments. But let justice run down like water, and righteousness like a mighty stream.'"

I *personally believe* that God is waiting for the church to bring about justice so that it runs down like water and righteousness runs like a mighty stream. Have you ever seen that in your life in the United States? When I read this passage, I have the feeling that loud worship, people gathering together to praise God, and a revival meeting simply won't do it anymore!

I asked the Lord if he will ever empty the mega churches, and if he would do it, how would he do it? I asked, "How will they become dinosaurs one day?" I *personally thought* I heard Jesus say that he will remove his presence from the buildings. They will meet, but no matter how much they're singing, his presence, his glory, and his anointing won't come.

Since writing this paragraph, a very close friend of mine who has read this manuscript said that is true of the church she attends. The church has thousands of people that come each week with multiple campuses, but my friend says that the presence of the Holy Spirit is not at that church.

I had a friend standing in church with me years ago. He said, "Do you think if the Holy Spirit left this building that the people would keep coming?"

And I said, "I don't know."

He said, "I think so. I don't think they'd recognize that the Holy Spirit is no longer here."

In that same meeting, I saw the worship leader go on and on, singing the same chorus over and over. She was pressing in, and the worship wasn't breaking through to the heavenlies. The Holy Spirit just wasn't breaking through. She sang this chorus over and over and over, and about the fifteenth time she sang it, his presence broke through, and the anointing hit the meeting. I don't think the audience knew that they hadn't broken through yet. They were just singing the song and wondering why she went on with the same chorus fifteen times. I *personally believe* that one day, in the future, many churches will worship God, and no matter how many songs they sing, the presence and anointing won't come.

I *personally believe*, as I have said several times, from my experience with Christians, a large majority of Christians can't hear Jesus speak to them. Yet Jesus said in John 10:22–30 that he's a good shepherd and his sheep hear his voice.

Now it was the Feast of Dedication in Jerusalem, and it was winter. And Jesus walked in the temple, in Solomon's porch. Then the Jews surrounded Him and said to Him, "How long do You keep us in doubt? If You are the Christ, tell us plainly."

Jesus answered them, "I told you, and you do not believe. The works that I do in My Father's name, they bear witness of Me. But you do not believe, because you are not of My sheep, as I said to you. My sheep hear My voice, and I know them, and they follow Me. And I give them eternal life, and they shall never perish; neither shall anyone snatch them out of My hand. My Father, who has given them to Me, is greater than all; and no one is able to snatch them out of My Father's hand. I and My Father are one."

Let me ask you a question. If you cannot hear Jesus's voice, do you personally think that are you actually his sheep?

Let me ask you another question. If you can't hear his voice and therefore can't follow what he tells you to do, are you really following him like he said his sheep would do?

I *personally feel* that Jesus is not after people to fill up church pews. Jesus is not after increased church attendance. He is after sheep, and by my reasoning, a large percentage of people who claim to be Christians cannot hear Jesus when he speaks. If you can't hear Jesus, how can you obey him?

When I preach that not all Christians are going to heaven, people quote this verse to me. "My Father who has given them to Me, is greater than all; and no one is able to snatch them out of My Father's hand" (John 10:29). People insist that you cannot lose your salvation because no one can snatch you out of the Father's hand.

That might be true. It might be true that true sheep cannot be snatched out of the Father's hand, but if you cannot hear Jesus speak, are you actually his sheep? This is vital for you to understand. You might be confessing that Jesus is your Lord, but this passage in Matthew 7:21–23 could apply to you.

"'Not everyone who says to Me, "Lord, Lord," shall enter the kingdom of heaven, but he who does the will of My Father in heaven. Many will say to Me in that day, "Lord, Lord, have we not prophesied in Your name, cast out demons in Your name, and done many wonders in Your name?" And then I will declare to them, "I never knew you; depart from Me, you who practice lawlessness!"'"

Many people don't understand that in this passage, Jesus spoke about people who were doing miracles with his anointing. They were saved, but they had departed from the right way. Many who believe in once saved, always saved cannot understand the clear warning in this passage from Jesus, because according to them, someone who is saved cannot go to hell.

You might be reading this and thinking, "I can't hear Jesus speak, but I don't believe that disqualifies me as a sheep. I go to church. I praise God. I live as a Christian. I am his follower, so I must be a sheep."

This passage also mentions a qualification for a sheep. You need to read this carefully and not just skim over it because I have known many people who confess Jesus as their Lord, but they do not do what this passage says that they should be doing with their lives. Matthew 25:31–45 puts it like this.

"When the Son of Man comes in His glory, and all the holy angels with Him, then He will sit on the throne of His glory. All the nations will be gathered before Him, and He will separate them one from another, as a shepherd divides his sheep from the goats. And He will set the sheep on His right hand, but the goats

on the left. Then the King will say to those on His right hand, 'Come, you blessed of My Father, inherit the kingdom prepared for you from the foundation of the world: for I was hungry and you gave Me food; I was thirsty and you gave Me drink; I was a stranger and you took Me in; I was naked and you clothed Me; I was sick and you visited Me; I was in prison and you came to Me.'

"Then the righteous will answer Him, saying, 'Lord, when did we see You hungry and feed You, or thirsty and give You drink? When did we see You a stranger and take You in, or naked and clothe You? Or when did we see You sick, or in prison, and come to You?' And the King will answer and say to them, 'Assuredly, I say to you, inasmuch as you did it to one of the least of these My brethren, you did it to Me.'

"Then He will also say to those on the left hand, 'Depart from Me, you cursed, into the everlasting fire prepared for the devil and his angels: for I was hungry and you gave Me no food; I was thirsty and you gave Me no drink; I was a stranger and you did *not take Me in, naked and you did not clothe Me, sick and in*

prison and you did not visit Me.'

"Then they also will answer Him, saying, 'Lord, when did we see

You hungry or thirsty or a stranger or naked or sick or in prison,

and did not minister to You?' Then He will answer them, saying,

'Assuredly, I say to you, inasmuch as you did not do it to one of

the least of these, you did not do it to Me.'

When you see a homeless stranger who is thirsty, hungry, or without (clean) clothes, how do you treat that man? Do you walk past him and his cardboard sign that says "Please help me."? Are you really a sheep, according to this passage of Scripture? Take a very honest look at this! If you don't hear Jesus speak and you are not a sheep, according to this passage, you need to change your ways and do so before you die.

Many of those who attend church would say that they are a son or a daughter of God. Let us have a look at what Paul says a son is. "For as many as are led by the Spirit of God, these are sons of God" (Romans 8:14).

I would *personally say* that very few Christians who attend church each week are led by the Spirit and walk in the Spirit. You might think that you are being led by the Holy Spirit each day, but can you personally tell the difference between a leading of the Holy Spirit and your own thought? If you cannot hear the Holy Spirit, how is he leading you each day? If you can't be led by the Holy Spirit, how would you survive the tribulation if Christians had to go through it? If those soldiers were walking up your street, going from door-to-door, and looking for Christians to collect and put into FEMA camps, could you hear the Holy Spirit clearly enough to walk right through the midst of them and trust that angels would hide you from them?

These are tough questions for you. Right about now, you might feel that this book is too tough and is very legalistic and that I am not preaching the truth as you understand it. What if this is actually the truth, and you have been following blind guides all your life? Don't you think Jesus was warning you in particular when he spoke of blind guides leading the blind? If this is shocking to you, might it be reasonable to consider that you have been blind to the truth?

You might get this book and show it to your leader and have him read it. He might become offended just as I might have offended you thus far with *my truth*. This passage in Matthew 15:12–14 might speak to that: "Then His disciples came and said to Him, 'Do You know that the Pharisees were offended when they heard this saying?' But He answered and said, 'Every plant which My heavenly Father has not planted will be uprooted. Let them alone. They are blind leaders of the blind. And if the blind leads the blind, both will fall into a ditch.'"

Where are you headed, dear reader? Do you really think the church, with its blind leaders, can honestly lead the world into a revival right now? The truth must be proclaimed, and the people of the churches must repent and change their ways. Are you starting to see why revival tarries?

I ask questions about passages that I read. I see a Scripture like this one in James 2:2–4. "For if there should come into your assembly a man with gold rings, in fine apparel, and there should also come in a poor man in filthy clothes, and you pay attention to the one wearing the fine clothes and say to him, 'You sit here in a good place,' and say to the poor man, 'You stand there,' or, 'Sit here at my footstool,' have you not shown partiality among yourselves, and become judges with evil thoughts?"

When you read a passage like that, you might not wonder what a friend of the world actually looks like. I read that I could be in a position where I am found to be an enemy of God, and it makes me wonder. I *personally consider* that over half of the church is friends with the world, and they have no idea that they are. Once again, a passage like this does not worry them because they mistakenly believe in once saved, always saved, and they think that they can serve both God and mammon. Jesus said very clearly that you cannot serve God and mammon at the same time, but the popular teaching in churches all around the world says that Jesus was mistaken, and you can, in fact, serve the world and God at the same time. "'No servant can serve two masters; for either he will hate the one and love the other, or else he will be loyal to the one and despise the other. You cannot serve God and mammon'" (Luke 16:13).

It is helpful to know that the word mammon can mean money and possessions. I have some questions for you.

What if a revival happened today? How would that change people? Would they suddenly become hot and not lukewarm anymore through a few revival meetings? Do you think you'll actually know all the commands of Jesus or suddenly hear Jesus speak after one revival meeting? Will you suddenly learn to be led by the Spirit? Do you think you will become obedient to Jesus, practiced in obedience, completely changed in your mind, and totally different after one revival meeting?

And do you think I'm being hard on you? Why have I bothered recording this video or writing this book? Why have I shared this message? This is why revival tarries. I *personally believe* that the church isn't ready or equipped. Churches aren't equipping their people; the church doesn't seem to know how to equip their people. By and large, the church is running ministries like businesses. They haven't told you this, in many cases, because they themselves are blind to the truth; they are not aware of this.

I've never heard any pastor preach on the commandments of Jesus when Jesus said, "If you love me, obey my commands." I've never heard any teacher in a church ever teach that. I heard one group of Christians teach about obeying Jesus. The church and internet called that group of Christians a cult. I learned a lot from that little cult on their website. You will have many interesting things to read if you check them out at Jesus Christians.

I loved that little so-called cult. I wrote them a letter years later, saying, "If any of your people need somewhere to stay, I have a spare bedroom in my house. They're welcome to stay with me." I love that group of people. They're the most full-on Christians I've never met. Now, years later, I am sounding pretty crazy myself. Much of what I am saying, people have not heard before.

What's a few stadiums? What will a few stadium meetings do? Will they transform you? What if you taught new Christians how to be like you? I'm talking to the people here that don't tithe, that don't give 10 percent of their income to God each week. I *personally believe* that's about 90 percent of you reading this book. How would you teach a new believer to hear God speak when over 80 percent of you cannot hear him? How will you teach a new convert to be led by the Spirit each day when most of you who are reading aren't led by the Spirit yourself? How will you teach people to be like Jesus when many of you don't know what he taught?

Jesus said in Matthew 15:8–9: "'These people draw near to Me with their mouth, and honor Me with their lips, but their heart is far from Me. And in vain they worship Me, teaching as doctrines the commandments of men.'"

When you have a heart for Jesus, you will want to obey him. When I have broached the subject about obeying the commandments of Jesus with some pastors, they have told me that trying to obey Jesus is a works doctrine. They have a doctrine of the finished works that says, in effect, all you have to do is accept Jesus, and your faith saves you and not anything that you do from that point on.

Here is an example of honoring Jesus with their lips but having a heart that is far from him. I had a woman close to my life up until yesterday that said she couldn't even wash the sandals that I wear. This really blessed me. I thought, "Wow, she seems like a really powerful prophet; why is she saying that to me?" Well, I didn't realize it was flattery; she was flattering me in front of the people I was leading. Within a week or two, I discerned that she had a Jezebel spirit that was trying to come in and control some of what I was doing online. When I told her what I had discerned in her and that I could not allow her to continue with us, the language and the emails changed drastically. I no longer had the impression that she wanted to wash my sandals!

You might be asking by now, "What's the point?" Until the church starts planting seeds and they have seeded the whole world, the Lord won't come and harvest it. Until the Christian church knows how to love and not be hypocrites by saying one thing and doing another in practice, God won't bring people to his church.

In Luke 6:46–49, Jesus said:

"But why do you call Me 'Lord, Lord,' and not do the things which I say? Whoever comes to Me, and hears My sayings and does them, I will show you whom he is like: He is like a man building a house, who dug deep and laid the foundation on the rock. And when the flood arose, the stream beat vehemently against that house, and could not shake it, for it was founded on the rock. But he who heard and did nothing is like a man

who built a house on the earth without a foundation, against which the stream beat vehemently; and immediately it fell. And the ruin of that house was great."

"Why do you call me Lord, Lord, and you do not do what I say?" It's easy to call Jesus, Lord, but is he really your Lord? A lord used to be a person in England who owned the estate and the land. Many people worked for him. People had their own positions and occupations, yet they all worked for the lord. He owned them.

Dictionary.com defines lord as follows:

Noun: 1. a person who has authority, control, or power over others; a master, chief, or ruler. 2. a person who exercises authority from property rights; an owner of land, houses, etc. 3. a person who is a leader or has great influence in a chosen profession.[7]

If Jesus is Lord over you, does Jesus own you?

Dictionary.com, s.v., "lord (*n* .)," Accessed February 16, 2019, ttps://www.dictionary.com/browse/lord.

If Jesus owns you and you do everything he says, ask him if you should send me a hundred dollars to prove it. You can find my ministry donation page here.

.

If you agree with this message, write to me at survivors.sanctuary@gmail.com and say, "I agree with the book called *Why Revival Tarries*, and I want to sow a hundred dollars into this ministry."

I was appalled when I found out that only 10 percent of people tithe, and 80 percent of people only sow 2 percent of their income, as I stated before. I was so shocked and saddened. This breaks my heart. I've wondered why I can't really watch many people preach, and for years, I had only been going to church for the fellowship. I wasn't going to church to learn anything.

How dare I say that I *personally believe* that 90 percent of Christians aren't led by the Holy Spirit? I know that the Holy Spirit can even lead Christians who cannot hear his voice. He can tell you to call your mom so that you have the idea to call her. You might call her, but you don't know the Holy Spirit told you. You might reach her on the phone and find out that she's been trying to call you with urgent news.

You just felt this inclination to call your mother, and you didn't know that the Holy Spirit was answering your mother's prayer so that you would call. The Holy Spirit can lead you to do things without your knowledge. The Holy Spirit doesn't need you to actually know that he is leading you to do things. The Holy Spirit moves in the lives of Christians but not because they know he's moving.

hope that the Holy Spirit has opened your eyes. I hope that you can see that you have some changes to make in your life and why the revival that will sweep the world before the return of Jesus is tarrying. If you have been convicted by this message and it has stirred you, I want you to send me a hundred dollars via PayPal. Write to me and tell me that you have read my book and that you agree with it.

would be excited to receive those emails along with your PayPal donations. This would really help my ministry, but more importantly, you might need to make an offering into this message. I really didn't even put the amount of a hundred dollars because I need your money. But when you sow into certain teachings and come into agreement with them, they can have a more powerful effect on your life.

I *personally think* that it wouldn't be the same if you just agreed with the message and didn't send the money. I feel that it would be very powerful if you prayed the following: "Lord, I want to change. Everything he said is true of me. I'm sorry for the way that I have lived my Christian life up to this point. Lead me to the truth. Teach me how to know these truths. Lead me to walk in your ways. Teach me how to walk in the Spirit. Show me your commands and help me obey them. Help me become a disciple. Help me witness to my friends and plant the seeds that need to be planted. I agree with his message. I will change. I've listened to this message and been convicted by it. I want to live it out. And as a sign of my desire to change, as a sign of my repentance, I will send him a hundred dollars."

I didn't make that up. The Holy Spirit gave me all the words in the video that this was taken from and helped me edit the words for the book. Your response is really up to you. I have a finance angel whose full-time job is to raise money for me, to put it on people's hearts to donate money to me. So I don't need your hundred dollars to publish books.

Every time I need money to publish a book, God miraculously provides it for me, no matter the amount. I might need two hundred dollars, five hundred dollars, a thousand dollars, or even five thousand dollars. No matter the amount, God sends it to me, often from completely unexpected sources. I really don't need your hundred dollars, because if you don't send it, someone else will. But do you *need* to send it?

The video that became this book was uploaded four weeks ago, and ninety people have viewed it. Four people were convicted enough to send my ministry hundred dollars. I told each of them that they didn't need to sow the money, and all of them insisted that they had to send me the money as they had made his promise to God.

You really need to be a light for people. We need to plant seeds of the gospel. As I previously stated, people have to hear the gospel five to six times on average *before* they can be saved. Again, the whole world has to hear the gospel five times before you bring them to the tent meeting, to the stadium, before they can be saved. In addition to hearing it six times, they have to find someone who actually lives out and demonstrates the Christian faith, who's proven their love for them.

I have written two books that will teach you more about this topic, *Influencing Your World for Christ* and *13 Tips to Becoming the Light of Christ*.

I might come to your city in twenty years. You might say, "Hey, that guy I always talk about is coming to town. I've been following him for twenty years.' Maybe I'll come to your town. Maybe you'll sow a thousand or two thousand dollars. You might do something else and build a great relationship with me. When I start getting invitations to the United States, I'll make sure to drop by your town and speak and save your friends.

I wrote a book called *7 Keys to Intimacy with Jesus*. I encourage you to read and apply it. I wrote another book called *How to Hear God's Voice*. Read and apply that book and learn how to hear God. I wrote another book called *Optimistic Visions of Revelation*. When you read and understand that book, you will learn and understand what will happen in the future and what I've seen.

personally believe that God won't use a bunch of hypocrites to save the world. When people cuss, they say, "Oh, Jesus. Oh, Christ. Oh, Jesus Christ." Do you know why Jesus Christ is a popular swear word? Do you know why the enemy tells people to use that word? Well, Jesus had the same problem. When he was on earth, Jesus told the Jews and the Jewish leaders that people blaspheme his Father's name because of them. He told them, "You're such hypocrites that they use my Father's name as a swear word."

Guess what? They're not using God the Father's name as a swear word anymore. They're using Jesus Christ. Do you know why? Because a whole bunch of hypocrites taught them that Jesus Christ has no power. People are swearing at Jesus because talk is cheap. They've heard Christians preach at them over and over, and no one's actually loving them with the love of Jesus.

Do you know what a hypocrite is? It's saying that you believe in something, but you don't do it. You use the word Christian and say that you're a Christian. A Christian means "little Christ." Are you a little Christ?

If you're in a foreign country or if something is preventing you from sending me a hundred dollars, I will pray for you all at the end of this message.

Jesus wants to say something:

Matthew doesn't need your money. You don't need me to bring a revival. You need to do what I told you to do in the Gospels. You need to build your house upon the rock. Most of you reading have built your house on the sand. If I came tonight, a lot of you would miss out on me taking you home, and you can't understand that now. If you died tonight, many of you reading this would not come to heaven.

In Revelation 3:16–17, I said, "So then, because you are lukewarm, and neither cold nor hot, I will vomit you out of My mouth. Because you say, 'I am rich, have become wealthy, and have need of nothing'—and do not know that you are wretched, miserable, poor, blind, and naked."

James 4:4 says this: "Adulterers and adulteresses! Do you not know that friendship with the world is enmity with God? Whoever therefore wants to be a friend of the world makes himself an enemy of God."

Here is one last Scripture for your consideration. "Do not love this world nor the things it offers you, for when you love the world, you do not have the love of the Father in you. 16 For the world offers only a craving for physical pleasure, a craving for everything we see, and pride in our achievements and possessions. These are not from the Father, but are from this world. 17 And this world is fading away, along with everything that people crave. But anyone who does what pleases God will live forever" (1 John 2:15–17, NLT).

These three scriptures I quoted give me the right not to bring disobedient Christians to heaven.

If you're lukewarm, if you're a friend of the world, you're not my bride. If you're not intimate with me, you won't make it to heaven. Many of you don't know me. You don't know me. Many of you prove you don't love me because you don't obey what I taught. (See John 14:15, 21, 23, and John 15:10.) You say you love me. You call me "Lord, Lord," but you don't do what I told you to do. I challenge you, send Matthew a hundred dollars and ask him to pray, and I'll move heaven and earth to get you into a place that'll fill your life with joy and with purpose.

I want you to know that I don't need your money. If you don't have the money, write to Matthew and ask him to pray for you. But I challenge you, donate toward this, sow into this, and share this message with your friends. Share this book with your friends on social media. Write to Matthew if you don't have the money. Say that you read this book and you agree with it and ask him to please pray for you.

I care for you; Matthew cares for you. I keep him up all night for a reason. Four weeks ago, the Holy Spirit told Matthew to stay up and not to sleep the night he did the video for this book. Matthew wanted to talk to his American friends. He sent a message to five of his friends over Facebook messenger, and as often happens, none of the messages went through to them right away. None of them received his messages or responded. He couldn't keep busy talking to friends, so he didn't know what to do. The Holy Spirit had told him to stay up, so he wanted to know what he was supposed to do with his time.

Then the Holy Spirit said to him, "Go to the toilet, shave, and make yourself presentable. Then come out and share that message, *Why*

Revival Tarries." He thought he was preparing for a thirty- or sixty-minute message. He had no idea it would be two hours long and that it would be another book. He simply had no idea. He really has no idea how long this will be. He's totally submitted. When he was speaking, he was fully submitted to the Holy Spirit and to me.

The Father speaks:

So who do you think you are? You use my name; you use my Son's name to finish your prayers. You say "in Jesus's name," but many of you don't even know my Son.

If you knew my Son, you'd obey him. If you were my Son's disciple, you'd look and act like my Son. You wouldn't be hiding your talent. Many of you don't even know my Son. You are so afraid: afraid of false prophets, of the Antichrist, of false teaching, and of being rejected by your friends if you share your faith with them. You're so afraid to share the gospel. You're so afraid to let go of your money and start investing in my kingdom. You don't trust me with your money.

Most of you don't trust me with your money. You don't trust me. I know who you are. I'm speaking to you. If you are reading this, I'm speaking to you. I know your sins. I know what you struggle with. I know all of you who are reading this book. I know which ones of you have decided within yourselves, "I'm not going to send the hundred dollars. I'm not going to write to him and say that I don't have enough money. I'm not going to share this book with my friends. I'm not going to repent."

I have to wonder, those of you who won't do those things, why did you read so far in this book? And should I even bother with you guys? Should I even bother with you? Why?

Why are you reading if you are not going to share this message, if you are not going to send the hundred dollars, and if you are not going to repent and change your ways? If you are not going to write to Matthew and say, "I don't have the money, but I agree with the message. Please pray for me." If you won't share this with your friends, why should I even speak to you anymore? You have to ask yourself that question. If you've read this far and refused to share, refused to sow, or refused to repent, why should I bother with you?

But for those people who will repent and who will write and share, I don't need you to share this message. Neither does Matthew. We're not asking you to share it so that Matthew becomes popular. I'm asking you to share it to save some of your friends from an eternity without me.

Sadly, even if you know this is God the Father speaking, perhaps you're more fearful of what your friends will think.

You might be afraid of your friends and what they'll think. They might be thinking about this, "Why did he share this? Who is this lunatic? Why did he think I should listen to this message?" What do you think your friends will think of you if you share this message with them?

In Mark 8:38, my Son said: "If anyone is ashamed of me and my message in these adulterous and sinful days, the Son of Man will be ashamed of that person when he returns in the glory of his Father with the holy angels."

Those that deny my Son before men, Jesus will deny when he comes. If you agree with this message, why don't you share it?

Do you care about any of your friends? Are you going to share this with them? If you're reading this on a Kindle or as a paperback, will you buy a copy for your friends? Matthew doesn't need the money from your purchase. He doesn't need your friends to hear this message. He doesn't need this book to become a bestseller. He doesn't need you to do anything.

I want to impress on you that this isn't a clever sales message. Matthew hasn't planned this message to ask you for a hundred dollars and then pretended to have Jesus ask you and then pretended to have me ask you. This isn't a clever marketing tool. Matthew doesn't use clever marketing techniques. He just says what we tell him to say. In fact, he had to consult with his best friends about even keeping this appeal for a hundred dollars in the book. He is really humbled before me to ask you for a hundred dollars.

Can you honestly do what we tell you to do? I want you to share the link to this Kindle book with your friends on social media. I want every one of you who've listened to this and been convicted by it to share it. I want every one of you to share it if you want to go to the next level and want to be included in Matthew's prayer.

I want every one of you to send a hundred dollars if you can afford it. If you are in a poor country like India, Africa, or China and a hundred dollars will break you, don't send the money. I know who can afford the money and who is blatantly rejecting our words and directions. If you are in the West, I want you to save up and send Matthew a message along with the money. I want you to send him a hundred dollars and then write to Matthew. Say, "I listened to *Why Revival Tarries*. I was convicted by it. Please pray for me." That's what I want you to do.

That's why revival tarries. We need the church body to stop being hypocrites, and we need to find Philadelphian pastors who know enough to equip their churches to be able to receive and love people into wholeness that we bring. We need time to prepare the church because the church needs a total reformation and a total rework. That can't be done in the next two years or even in the next five years. We need time.

Whether you believe it or not, Matthew has to fulfill all the prophecies that have been spoken over his life. That will take at least twenty years.

You might also remember the Indian apostle that needs to plant fifteen hundred churches with only six hundred so far. So that's why revival tarries. We're waiting; we're building the framework, the people, the churches, and the support to handle the harvest. We need all of you who are listening to this message, all of you who are reading this book, to shine your light and sow seeds for the harvest.

We don't even mind if you save a few people. I love you. I do love you, even those of you who refuse to accept this message. I love you. It wasn't Matthew's idea to preach a message of heavy conviction. We just called him to speak this way. He loves you too. I am finished now. So I will let Matthew wrap it up.

(Matthew speaks again.)

When I said that Jesus and the Father spoke, I hope that you recognized that they were speaking. To close out this book, I will pray for you. I really admire you if you read this entire book up to this point. If you cannot afford to give to my ministry, this is for you.

Dear Father,

I want to pray for the people: those who are touched and inspired by this message, those who do or don't respond and ask me for a prayer, those who do or don't share the message, and those who don't respond how you told them to respond.

I pray that your Holy Spirit would be with them and lead them into all truth. "When the Spirit of truth comes, he will guide you into all truth. He will not speak on his own but will tell you what he has heard. He will tell you about the future" (John 16:13).

I pray that over the coming weeks, months, and years that you will bring confirmation of this message through many sources and confirm its validity and truth.

Please lead them to the books, teachers, pastors, and those who can confirm that this message was the truth. I pray that no matter how long it takes them to respond and send their money or to write and ask me to pray, that I will still respond to them. I pray that no matter how long it takes for them to really repent and change their ways and start working toward the right way of living, that you'll stay with them, lead them, direct them, be with them, and save them. I pray that I'll see every one of the people who agree with this message in heaven.

Please let all the readers who are affected by this come up to me in heaven. I pray that everyone who hears these words and who agrees with this message will come up to me in heaven and thank me for this book.

Please be with each of the readers. Turn them into true sheep, save them, and bless them. Refine them, chastise them, and do whatever you need in their lives, dear Jesus, until they know how to build their house on the rock.

I pray that you keep them all safe. Please remind them and bring confirmation from all over the place that this message is true—through many teachers in many different ways, the ads on buses, songs on the radio, and people that they meet.

I pray that you would remove anything I said that was error from the message as a stumbling block and discount it. Work with the people and guide them into truth, even if they doubt some of my words. Please work and confirm this word.

Please persist for years and years and years until people understand that they have read the truth and have them respond. Even if they send their hundred dollars in ten years or if they can't afford it, they can message or email me and ask for prayer. Please bring every person with an open heart to yourself.

I pray for all these people. Lord, be with them, bless them, and lead them into all truth. Once again, please cancel anything I said that wasn't the truth. In Jesus's name, I ask. Amen.

If you were touched and convicted by this message, please email me or send me a friend request on Facebook. If you send me a friend request on Facebook, please get in touch with me via Messenger.

When I tell you how to respond, it is like an altar call. Sometimes during an altar call, you just feel too nervous to go forward and publicly shame and humble yourself. You say, "Lord, I repent, and I agree with this message. But please forgive me in my seat so that I don't have to go forward." If that's you, if you can't do what you've been told to do, I pray for you, too, like I prayed for everyone else. I pray that the Lord would pour out his love and lead you to truth. I really do love you. I don't even know you, but I know that the Lord loves you.

God obviously had something to say because this message lasted so long. Some will say that this was a hard message, and some of your friends might think you're crazy if you share this. But wouldn't it be good if ten of your friends shared it and then ten of those people shared it? What if it went from ten to a hundred to a thousand and became an exponential explosion? Wouldn't that be a wonderful result?

May God bless you and keep you.

Matthew Robert Payne

December 21, 2018

I'D LOVE TO HEAR FROM YOU

One of the ways that you can bless me as a writer is by writing an honest and candid review on Amazon of my book. I always read the reviews of my books, and I would love to hear what you have to say about this one.

Before I buy a book, I read the reviews first. You can make an informed decision about a book when you have read enough honest reviews from readers. One way to help me sell this book and to give me positive feedback is by writing a review for me. It doesn't cost you a thing but helps me and the future readers of this book enormously.

To read my blog, request a life-coaching session, request your own personal prophecy, or receive a personal message from your angel, you can also visit my website at http://personal-prophecy-today.com. All of the funds raised through my ministry website will go toward the books that I write and self-publish.

To write to me about this book or to share any other thoughts, please feel free to contact me at my personal email address at survivors.sanctuary@gmail.com.

You can also friend request me on Facebook at Matthew Robert Payne. Please send me a message if we have no friends in common as a lot of scammers now send me friend requests. I am starting a community church meeting on Zoom and training people in the prophetic over the Zoom platform, so make sure you get in touch with me to be part of that.

You can also do me a huge favor and share this book on Facebook as a recommended book to read, which will help me and other readers.

HOW TO SPONSOR A BOOK PROJECT

I f you have been blessed by this book, you might consider sponsoring a book for me. It normally costs me between fifteen hundred and two thousand dollars or more to produce each book that I write, depending on the length of the book. If you seek the Holy Spirit about financing a book for me, I know that the Lord would be eternally grateful to you.

Consider how much this book has blessed you and then think of hundreds or even thousands of people who would be blessed by a book of mine. As you are probably aware, the vast majority of my e-books cost ninety-nine cents, which proves to you that book writing is indeed a ministry for me and not a money-making venture. I would be very happy if you supported me in this. If you have any questions for me or if you want to know what projects I am currently working on that your money might finance, you can write to me at survivors.sanctuary@gmail.com and ask me for more information. I would be pleased to give you more details about my projects.

You can sow any amount to my ministry by simply sending me money via the PayPal link at this address: http://personal-prophecy-today.com/support-my-ministry.

You can be sure that your support, no matter the amount, will be used for the publishing of helpful Christian books for people to read.

Suggested further reading

Intoxicated with Babylon by Steve Gallagher

Standing Firm through the Great Apostasy by Steve Gallagher

Driven by Eternity by John Bevere

Influencing Your World for Christ by Matthew Robert Payne

13 Tips to Becoming the Light of Christ by Matthew Robert Payne

Optimistic Visions of Revelation by Matthew Robert Payne

Prophetic Evangelism Made Simple by Matthew Robert Payne

How to Hear God's Voice by Matthew Robert Payne

Divine Healing Made Simple by Praying Medic

You can find many other books by Matthew Robert Payne at his Amazon home page.

Acknowledgments

Jesus:

I want to thank you for being my lifelong friend and for never deserting me, no matter how dark my life became. You have led me into some great adventures. Being with you has filled my life with meaning.

Holy Spirit:

I want to thank you for leading and teaching me. You are a great teacher, better than I could ever be. You have been with me every step of the way. Thank you for your help with this book. You practically dictated it.

Father:

Thank you for loving me and entrusting me with this life that I am living. Thank you for revealing my purpose to me and leading me toward accomplishing it. Thank you so much for your Son, Jesus. Thank you for everything that you have done in my life. Thank you for leading me to help more people with another book. Thank you for your words in this book.

Lisa Thompson:

I want to especially thank Lisa for editing this book of mine. You take my simple words and transform them to make me seem smarter than I really am.

If you have any editing needs, you can contact Lisa at

writebylisa@gmail.com.

Nicola:

I want to thank Nicola for being part of my team as a proofreader and for writing the foreword for this book. I want to thank you for all the work that you did with this book to polish and improve it. I love every phone call I have with you. You can contact Nicola, my dear friend, for your own personal prophecy on my website.

Friends:

I want to thank Darla, Lisa, Nicola, Mary, Wendy, David Joseph, Michael Van Vlymen, David, Tufan, Andy, Jinny, and Ruth for your friendship and for how you have impacted my life.

Mom and Dad:

I want to thank my mother and father for all the love that they have given me. I am a product of your love.

Readers and ministry supporters:

I want to thank the readers of my books and my ministry supporters for the funds that you have given me to publish books. I live to educate people, and I thank my readers and the supporters of my ministry because you make life worth living.

Matthew Robert Payne, a teacher and prophet, enjoys writing what the Lord puts on his heart to share. He receives great pleasure from interacting with others on Facebook, hearing from people who have read his books, and prophesying over people's lives. He is a passionate lover of and disciple of Jesus Christ. He hopes that as you discover his books, you will intimately come to know Jesus, the Father, and Matthew through his transparent writing style.

Matthew grew up in a traditional Baptist church and gave his heart to Jesus Christ at the tender age of eight years old. But he left home at the age of eighteen, living a wild life for many years and engaging in bad habits and addictions. At twenty-seven, he was baptized in water and, at the same time, baptized in the Holy Spirit. Matthew learned about the five-fold ministry offices and received a revelation of their value today.

He started his journey as a prophet twenty years ago, learning about this gift and putting it into practice. With thousands of prophecies under his belt, he can confidently prophesy to friends and strangers alike. He has been writing for a number of years and self-published his first book in

2011. Today he spends his time earning money to self-publish and writes a new book approximately every month. You can find sixteen hundred of his videos on YouTube under Matthew Robert Payne.

You can connect with him on Facebook. You can sow into his book-writing ministry, read his blog, receive a message from your angel, or even receive your own nine-minute personal prophecy from Matthew at http://personal-prophecy-today.com.

Blurb

For decades, many prophetic words have been released, promising revival to the world. Some of these declarations even include numbers, such as "the billion-soul revival." Most Christians firmly believe that these prophecies are accurate, so they sit back and wait for the coming revival, praying that it will happen soon. But what if we need to do much more than just wait and pray?

In *Why Revival Tarries*, Matthew Robert Payne addresses possible reasons for the delay of the coming revival. But rest assured, you will be surprised at the reasons he lists. Hint: This delay has nothing to do with the unsaved.

After listing some of these reasons, this powerful and convicting book wraps up with a word from Jesus and a word from God the Father for the reader. So fasten your seat belt and hang on tight! Prepare for a wild ride and enjoy the journey!

www.ingramcontent.com/pod-product-compliance
Lightning Source LLC
Chambersburg PA
CBHW021936040426
42448CB00008B/1087